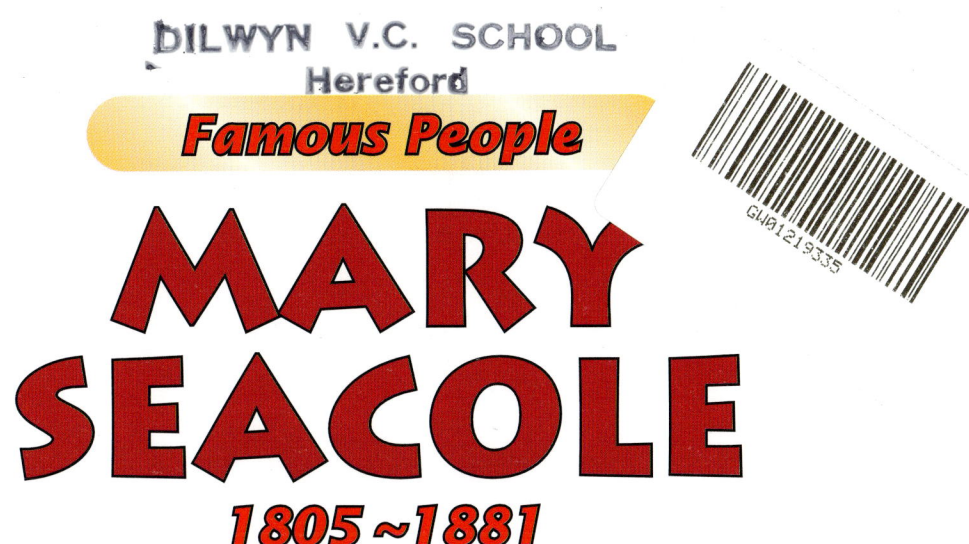

Famous People

MARY SEACOLE
1805~1881

Christine Moorcroft
Magnus Magnusson

Christine Moorcroft is an educational consultant and an Ofsted inspector, who was a teacher in primary and special schools and a lecturer in education. She has written and edited several books on history and religion and on other subjects, including personal and social education, science and English.

Magnus Magnusson KBE, has written several books on history and archaeology, and translated many Icelandic sagas and modern Icelandic novels. He has presented major television programmes on history and archaeology, such as *Chronicle*, *The Archaeology of the Bible Lands* and *Living Legends*, as well as the long-running quiz series, *Mastermind*. He is currently chairman of Scottish Natural Heritage, the Government body which advises on environmental issues.

ACKNOWLEDGEMENTS

The authors thank the following for their help: Alex Attewell (Curator, Florence Nightingale Museum, St Thomas' Hospital, London); Sam Walker (Director, Black Cultural Archive, Brixton, London).

Picture credits
Mary Evans Picture Library: pages 4 (Jamaica then), 5 (both), 7, 8, 11, 12 (top), 13 (bottom), 14 (bottom), 15,
National Library of Jamaica: page 19 (both)
Florence Nightingale Museum: pages 12 (bottom), (14 top), 18 (both)
Jamaica Tourist Board: page 4 (Jamaica today)
The Wellcome Trust: page 13 (top)

Published by Channel Four Learning Limited
Castle House
75–76 Wells Street
London W1P 3RE

© 1998 Channel Four Learning

All rights reserved.

Written by Christine Moorcroft and Magnus Magnusson
Illustrated by Michelle Ives
Cover illustration by Jeffrey Burn
Designed by Blade Communications
Edited by Margot O'Keeffe
Printed by Alden Press
ISBN 1-86215-349-3

For further information about Channel 4 Schools and details of published materials, contact
Channel 4 Schools
PO Box 100
Warwick CV34 6TZ
Tel: 01926 436444
Fax: 01926 436446

Contents

Jamaica	4
Growing up in Kingston	6
Travel and marriage	8
Helping the sick	10
To the battlefields	12
The Crimea	14
The 'British Hotel'	16
'Mother Seacole' retires	18
Time-lines	20
How to find out more	22
Glossary	23
Index	24

Jamaica

Jamaica is an island in the Caribbean Sea. The people who lived there from about AD600 were called the Arawaks. They called the island 'Xaymaca', which means 'land of many springs'. They lived on crops, such as corn and cassava, and by fishing.

There are no Arawaks left today. Many were killed in 1509 when Spain invaded the island. Others died from infections which they caught from the Spanish settlers. The settlers grew plantations of sugar, citrus fruits and bananas.

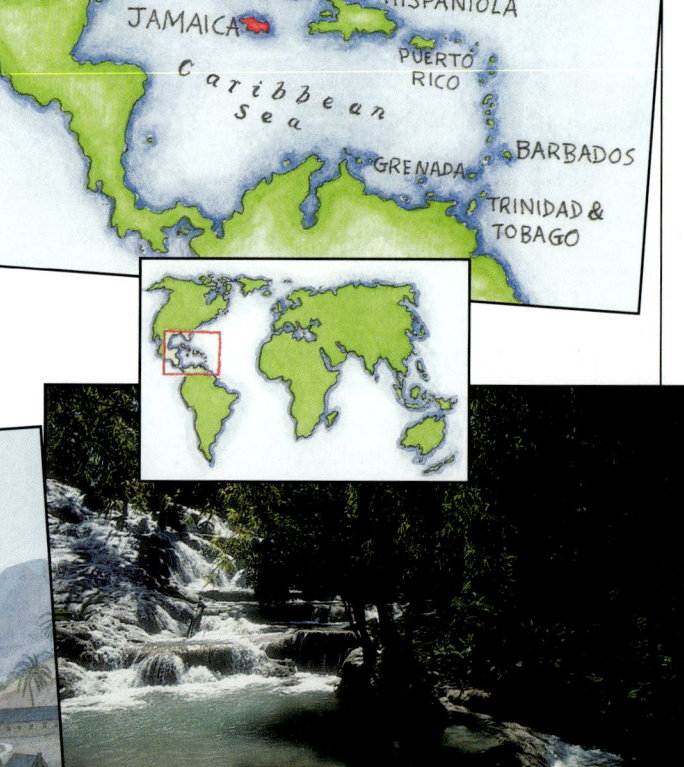

A map of the Caribbean.

Pictures of Jamaica in Mary Seacole's time and today.

Slaves working in a sugar refinery in Jamaica.

In 1655 Britain captured Jamaica from Spain. By this time there were not many people left in Jamaica, so the people who owned the plantations had to bring in workers from other lands. Some came from Europe and others were prisoners from British jails. But there were still not enough workers.

That is when the slave trade began. Ships from Africa brought slaves for work on the plantations. Some slaves were just given food and somewhere to live. Others had land around their huts on which they grew crops and kept animals for food and for sale. After years of slavery some, like Mary Seacole's mother, gained their freedom.

Slaves celebrating their freedom in Jamaica in 1838.

Did you know?

- **When Mary was growing up in Jamaica there were still slaves working on the plantations.**
- *A plantation is a large farm.*
- *The slave trade ended in 1834. Slavery ended in 1838.*

Growing up in Kingston

Mary was born in Kingston, Jamaica, in 1805. Her mother had been a slave, from Africa, who had gained her freedom. She had worked hard growing vegetables on her small piece of land and had saved up enough money to buy an inn.

At that time there were many British soldiers and sailors in Kingston. Mary's mother had married a Scottish officer. They had three children – Mary, Edward and Louisa.

Mary's mother had learned to use the herbs which grew in Jamaica to treat illnesses. She often looked after the British officers and their wives who stayed in Kingston.

Blundell Hall, the inn run by Mrs Grant, Mary's mother, in East Street, Kingston.

A drawing of Kingston, Jamaica, from Mary Seacole's time.

Mary often watched her mother looking after sick and wounded officers. She played at being a doctor, giving her dolls mixtures she had made from herbs. She bandaged their arms, legs and heads, just as her mother did to real patients. By the time she was 12 she was helping her mother to treat her patients.

- Never play with medicines. Only take medicines from an adult you trust.

Mary learned from the hotel guests about other countries. The soldiers and sailors would tell her tales of travel and battles. She wanted to see the world for herself. She often looked at a map of the world and traced the route to Britain, her father's country. She wanted to go there first.

Mary as a little girl.

Did you know?

- *Jamaica was ruled by Britain in Mary's time.*
- *Kingston was a big port, and the capital city of Jamaica.*
- *Soldiers as well as sailors went from Britain to Jamaica by sea.*
- *There were no aeroplanes.*

Travel and marriage

When Mary was 12 she went to England with some of her relatives. She stayed in London for a year. She was called names by other children because she was black. Nonetheless, she went back to London many times.

In November 1825, on her way way back to Jamaica from another trip to England, the ship caught fire! Mary promised to pay the ship's cook two pounds if he would tie her to his big hen-coop which would help her to float if the ship sank!

Happily, the fire was put out and the ship arrived safely in Kingston in February 1826. Mary was 20 years old at that time.

Soon after her voyages to England, Mary sailed to the other Caribbean islands to see what she could buy and sell. From New Providence in the Bahamas she brought back beautiful shells and objects made from them, which she soon sold.

This ship is like the one in which Mary travelled from Jamaica to England.

8

Mary learned a lot about medicine by helping the doctors.

After her travels Mary stayed at her mother's inn. She learned a lot about using herbs for medicine. She met an English officer called Horatio Edwin Seacole who was staying at the inn. They fell in love and were married. Sadly, before long he became very ill. Mary nursed him, but he died. Soon afterwards Mary's mother died, too.

Mary married an English army officer.

Mary became well-known as what Jamaicans called a 'doctress'. The inn was always full of sick army officers. When army doctors stayed there, Mary learned from them about medicine and surgery. When one woman died from cholera, Mary helped the doctor who treated her. She found out as much as she could about this dreadful disease.

Did you know?

- Many Jamaican women were 'doctresses'. They grew herbs in what they called 'balmyards'.

- They had no training in medicine, but they learned how to use the herbs which grew on the island. They could treat wounds and broken bones.

Helping the sick

In 1850 Mary went to Panama, where her brother, Edward, had opened a shop and a hotel. She took her medicine chest.

While she was there, a friend of her brother became very ill and died within a few days. Mary knew that he had died of cholera. At first nobody believed her. Then a friend of the dead man also became ill. Mary treated him and he recovered.

Many more people began to suffer from the same disease. There was no doctor, and so they went to Mary for help. Even the doctor who was sent to help could see that Mary knew how to treat people with cholera.

One night a baby whom Mary had tried to save died from cholera. She wanted to learn more about the disease and so she cut open the little body to examine it before burying it. Later she wrote that this helped her to understand cholera and to save other people's lives.

Mary helped more and more people when they became ill.

A picture of a battle during the Crimean War.

In 1854 Britain and France went to war against Russia in a place called the Crimea. Mary wanted to go to there to nurse the sick and wounded soldiers.

She went to London to offer to go to the Crimea as a nurse. She took with her letters from doctors who knew about her work. But wherever she tried she was turned away. She had heard about Florence Nightingale's nurses and went to see if she could join them.

Mary was told that no more nurses were needed. She went back to her lodgings in tears.

The Crimea.

Did you know?

- *The war in 1854 became known as the Crimean War because it took place in an area called the Crimea.*

- *Florence Nightingale was a well-known nurse who was also in the Crimea.*

To the battlefields

Mary decided that nobody was going stop her from going to the battlefields. She paid her own fare to get to the Crimea. She planned how to make a living while she was there.

Mary had read in the newspapers about the soldiers' poor food and their cold, uncomfortable camps in the Crimea. She sent cards to the army officers she knew there to let them know that she was coming to set up a 'British Hotel'. She said it would be comfortable for the sick and wounded officers.

Below is William Russell who wrote about the war for The Times newspaper.

Left is a painting of a battle in which the soldiers were wounded.

On 25th January 1855, Mary set off for the Crimea with stores of food and other useful things to sell. A steamship took her to the coast of Turkey, which is across the Black Sea from the Crimea.

Florence Nightingale was in charge of the army hospital at Scutari in Turkey.

A painting from the time of Florence Nightingale looking after the wounded in the hospital.

Mary went to see her and she was given a bed for the night.

At the hospital, Mary helped in the wards as much as she could. Some of the patients were soldiers she had known in Jamaica.

A painting of the hospital and its grounds, with the graves of many of the soldiers who had died.

Did you know?

- There had been no female nurses in army hospitals until Florence Nightingale took her nurses to Scutari in Turkey.

13

The Crimea

Sick and wounded soldiers being ferried to hospital.

On the very day Mary sailed into Balaclava, some sick and wounded soldiers were brought there from the battlefields on the way to the hospital. Mary set to work at once, cleaning and bandaging their wounds, giving them tea and treating them with her medicines.

Mary had nowhere to stay, so she was given a bed on a ship in the harbour. Each night she would climb up a ladder running up the side of the ship. She had her goods stacked on the quay, where it was difficult to keep them safe from thieves. There she sat and, when she was not looking after wounded soldiers, she sold things from her stores.

Above is a picture of Balaclava harbour during the Crimean War.

After six weeks at Balaclava, Mary decided to build a shop at a place called Spring Hill.

It was not easy to find building materials and builders, but at last the shop was built. It was just a large hut but it would be her home, as well as a shop and a place where travellers could buy food and drinks.

This painting from the Crimean war shows army supplies on the way to the camps.

Mrs Seacole's Hut.

'Mrs Seacole's Hut' soon became very well known. It was even marked on some of the war maps. The soldiers often called her 'Mother Seacole' because she looked after them like a mother.

Did you know?

- *The roads were just tracks. They were dusty in hot weather and muddy when it rained.*
- *People travelled on horseback or in a horse-drawn carriage or cart.*
- *There was a railway to the army camp.*

15

The 'British Hotel'

In 1855 Mary built the 'British Hotel' at Spring Hill. The main building was a long room with counters, cupboards and shelves. Nearby there were wooden buildings in which Mary and the hotel workers slept, and a canteen for the soldiers. In the yard there were huts for animals.

Inside the 'British Hotel'.

These French soldiers are called Zouaves. Mary thought they hid stolen goods in their baggy trousers.

Mary had problems. Rats nibbled their way into the sacks and barrels of food in the store. They even attacked a live sheep and bit the cook! Thieves stole 40 goats and seven sheep, as well as dozens of geese and turkeys. Mary was sure the thieves were the soldiers who wore huge baggy trousers and could hide things inside them.

In June 1855 Mary heard that the British army was going to attack Sebastopol. She spent a whole night, with her cooks and other workers, cutting bread and cheese, making sandwiches and packing cooked ham and chicken, wines and spirits. She filled her medicine bag with lint, bandages, medicines, needles and thread. By daybreak it was all loaded on to two mules, and off she rode to the battlefield.

During the battles Mary did not wait for the 'all-clear' before picking her way through the dead and injured men, looking for any to help. Sometimes there was a shout of "Lie down, mother, lie down!" She had to fling herself face down on to the ground for safety as a cannon-ball landed nearby.

Mary tended the wounded men in the Crimea.

Did you know?

- *Many people who were in the Crimea remembered seeing Mary Seacole near the scenes of battles, with her stove and kettle, making tea for the soldiers. She paid for this herself.*

'Mother Seacole' retires

On 11 September, Sebastopol was taken from the Russians. The guards were not supposed to let anyone except soldiers into the city. But they recognised Mary and let her go in. She took food and drink for the soldiers.

But the war was not over, and Mary worked hard that winter to prepare for Christmas visitors to her hotel.

Army officers at Christmas in 1855.

A drawing, from the Crimean War, showing soldiers' graves near the harbour at Balaclava.

In March 1856 the war ended. Mary's hotel and shop, on which she had spent all her money, were no longer needed. She packed as many of her things as she could for the journey back. She visited the graves of some of the soldiers she had known. Mary sailed to England. She had no money left.

Mary was famous when she arrived in London. People had read about her in the newspapers. She was the guest of honour at a dinner with the army. The soldiers cheered her.

They held a 'Grand Military Festival' to raise money for her. Many people gave her money. Mary thought of a way to make some money for herself – she wrote her life story! It was called 'The Wonderful Adventures of Mrs Seacole in Many Lands.'

A sculpture of Mary Seacole.

She still treated people with her medicines and did a lot of work to help war widows and orphans. She died in London on 14 May 1881. She was buried at St Mary's Catholic Cemetery in Kensal Rise, London.

Medals awarded to Mary for the work she did in the Crimean War.

Did you know?

- *Queen Victoria gave money to Mary.*
- *Mary left most of her money to her sister, Louisa (Edward, her brother, had died in Panama).*
- *To people who had helped her, she left money, jewellery and other possessions.*

Time-lines

Mary went to England for the first time

The slave trade was banned

Mary married Horatio Edw Seacole

1805 **1817/18** **1834 1836**

Mary was born

55
Julius Caesar invaded Britain

c30
Jesus was crucified

c570
Muhammad was born

500BC　　　　　　　　　0　　　　　　　　　AD500

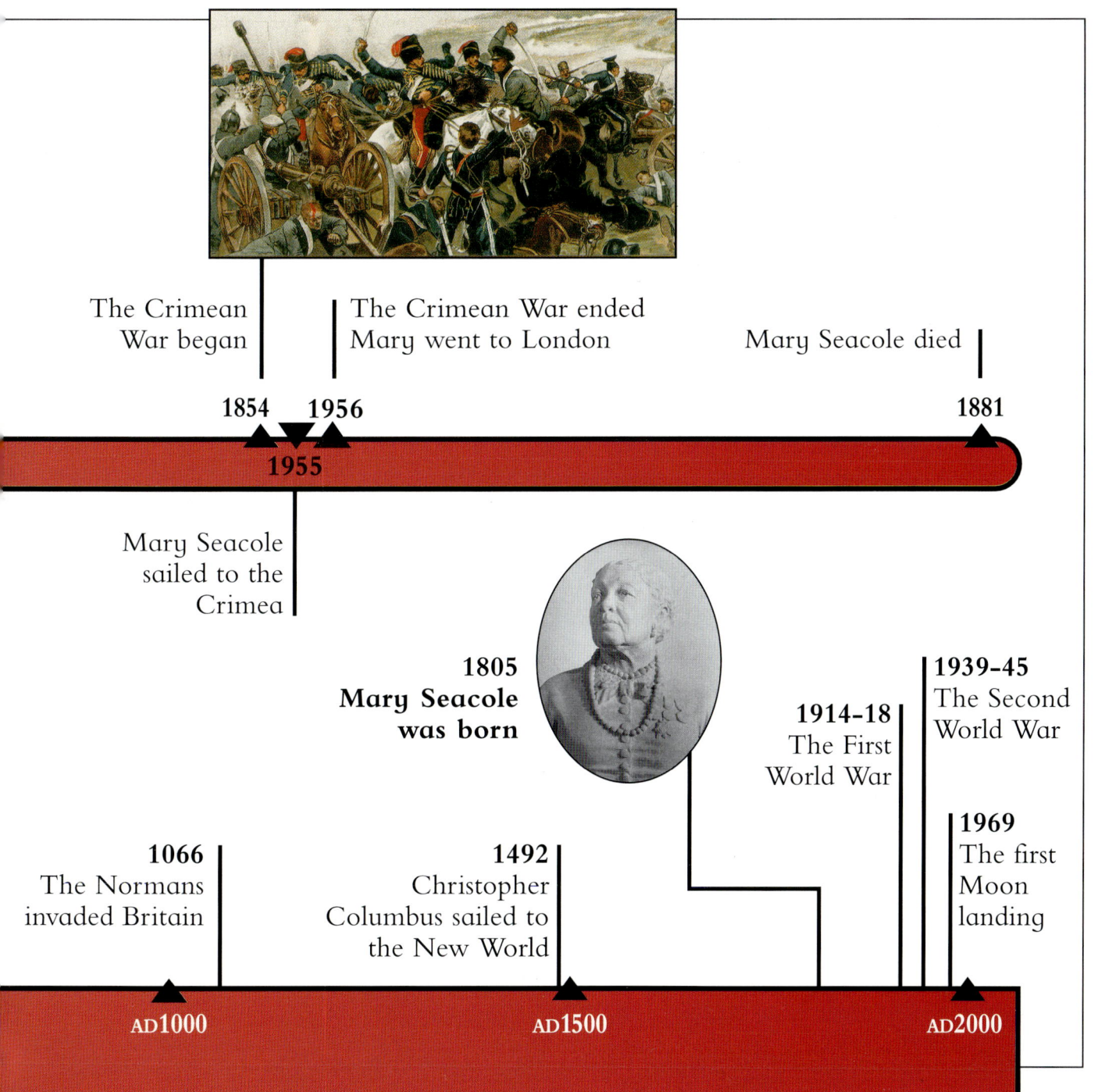

21

How to find out more

More books to read

The Crimean War by Paul Kerr and others (Channel 4, 1997)

The Florence Nightingale Museum's School Visit Pack by V Woollard (Florence Nightingale Museum, 1997)

Two Lives, Florence Nightingale and Mary Seacole by Eric L Luntley (Bogle-L'Ouverture Press, 1993)

Mary Seacole Teacher's Pack by M Hussey & S Walker (Black Cultural Archive, The Florence Nightingale Museum, London, 1992)

The Wonderful Adventures of Mrs Seacole in Many Lands by Z Alexander & A Dewjee (Editors) (Falling Wall Press, 1984)

Television programmes to watch

Channel 4 Schools series, Stop Look, Listen: Famous People. Telephone 01926 436444.

Places to visit or to which to write

Black Cultural Archive, 378 Coldharbour Lane, Brixton, London SW9 8LF. Tel 0171 738 4591.

Florence Nightingale Museum, St Thomas' Hospital, 2 Lambeth Palace Road, London SE1 7EW. Tel 0171 620 0374, fax 0171 928 1760.

Museum of the Royal Pharmaceutical Society of Great Britain, 1 Lambeth High St, London SE1, 0171 735 9141.

Merseyside Maritime Museum (Emigrants to the New World Exhibition), Albert Dock, Liverpool L3 4AQ. Tel 0151 478 4499.

National Army Museum, Royal Hospital Road, London SW3 4HT. 0171 730 0717.

Science Museum (Wellcome History of Medicine Galleries), Exhibition Road, London SW7 2DD. Tel 0171 938 9000.

Glossary

Arawak *(4)* Native people living in Jamaica (AD600–1509).

balmyard *(9)* A herb-garden. This word was used mainly in tropical countries like Jamaica.

camps *(12)* A place where soldiers live, often in tents, during a war.

canteen *(16)* A room in which soldiers or workers eat.

cassava *(4)* A crop grown in tropical countries. Its tubers can be ground into flour.

cholera *(9)* (pronounced ko-ler-a). A disease from bacteria (germs).

citrus fruits *(4)* Fruits like orange, grapefruit, lemon and lime.

doctress *(9)* A woman who looked after people with injuries and illnesses, and used medicines made from herbs.

herbs *(6)* Plants used for cooking and medicines.

infections *(4)* Illnesses caused by germs.

invade *(4)* Attack a country to take it over.

military *(19)* Something done by, or for, soldiers.

orphan *(19)* A child whose parents are dead.

plantation *(4)* A large farm.

quay *(14)* A place where boats dock.

refinery *(5)* A building in which raw sugar is cleaned.

route *(7)* The course taken by travellers.

settlers *(4)* People who move from one place to live in another.

slave *(5)* A worker owned by an employer and who was not paid.

slavery *(5)* Buying and selling people as unpaid workers.

Zouave *(16)* A French-Algerian soldier.

Index

Africa, 5, 6,

Arawak, 4

army, 6–7, 9, 11–9

Balaclava, 11, 14, 15, 18

battles, 12-15, 17

Blundell Hall, 6

Britain and the British, 5, 6, 7, 8, 11

British Hotel, 12, 16, 18

Caribbean, 4, 8

cholera, 9, 10

Crimea, 11-19

Edward (Mary Seacole's brother), 6, 10, 19

France and the French, 11, 16

Jamaica, 4–9, 13

Kingston, capital of Jamaica, 6, 7, 8

London, 8, 11, 19

Louisa (Mary Seacole's sister), 6, 19

Nightingale, Florence, 11, 13

Panama, 10, 19

plantations, 4, 5

Russell, William, 12

Russia, 11, 18

Scutari, 13

Seacole, Horatio Edwin (Mary Seacole's husband), 9

Sebastopol, 11, 17, 18

slaves and slavery, 5–6

Spain and the Spanish, 4, 5

Spring Hill, 15, 16

Turkey, 11, 13